THE
COMPLETE CLERIHEWS
OF
E. CLERIHEW BENTLEY

'here for another generation of connoisseurs of highly literate idiocy is the whole exquisite, tiny *oeuvre* . . . The fine pen drawings of Victor Reinganum and Nicolas Bentley complement Chesterton's illustrations to complete this elegantly designed, altogether delightful book, which will fit neatly into gentlemen's pockets, ladies' handbags and the Christmas stockings of precociously erudite children.' *Spectator*

This is a collection of all the clerihews published by E. C. Bentley, and it includes all the original illustrations that helped them charm their way into the affections of countless readers. Inconsequential, often anachronistic, always biographical, these benignly satirical and absurdly amusing verses have been so wholeheartedly adopted in the literary world that their name has become part of our language. The poet Gavin Ewart, a long-standing devotee of humorous verse, introduces this unique collection with an account of Bentley and of clerihews in general. For this new edition he has added a passage about the recently discovered school notebook in which Bentley recorded the original clerihews (mostly unpublished) written by himself and his friends as teenagers. (This notebook has now been published in facsimile by Oxford University Press as *The First Clerihews*.) He also quotes two additional Bentleian 'throw-outs', one with a Nicolas Bentley illustration.

The new edition contains other additions too: a longer clerihew-preface by the author (written originally for a new edition of *Biography for Beginners*), Nicolas Bentley's illustration for the jacket of *More Biography*, and a greatly expanded 'Index of Psychology' which now includes all the entries from the original books.

Gavin Ewart is also the compiler of *Other People's Clerihews*, an anthology of the best imitations inspired by Bentley's verses.

The COMPLETE

CLERIHEWS

of

E. CLERIHEW BENTLEY

Illustrated by

NICOLAS BENTLEY
G. K. CHESTERTON
VICTOR REINGANUM
and the Author

With an Introduction by

GAVIN EWART

Revised edition

Oxford   New York

OXFORD UNIVERSITY PRESS

1983

Oxford University Press, Walton Street, Oxford OX2 6DP

London Glasgow New York Toronto
Delhi Bombay Calcutta Madras Karachi
Kuala Lumpur Singapore Hong Kong Tokyo
Nairobi Dar es Salaam Cape Town
Melbourne Auckland

and associated companies in
Beirut Berlin Ibadan Mexico City Nicosia

Oxford is a trade mark of Oxford University Press

Introduction © Gavin Ewart 1981, 1983

First published as
Biography for Beginners (*1905*), More Biography (*1929*),
in Punch (*1938, 1939*)*, and in* Baseless Biography (*1939*)
First published in complete collected form by
Oxford University Press 1981
Reprinted 1981
Second edition published as an Oxford University Press paperback 1983

British Library Cataloguing in Publication Data

Bentley, E. Clerihew
The complete clerihews of E. Clerihew Bentley
—Rev. ed.—(Oxford paperbacks)
1. *English wit and humour*
I. Title II. Bentley, Nicolas
III. Chesterton, G.K. IV. Reinganum, Victor
828'. 91209 PN6175
ISBN 0-19-281391-9

Printed in Great Britain by
Richard Clay (The Chaucer Press) Ltd.
Bungay, Suffolk

Contents

Biography for Beginners
Deals with various saints and sinners,
And the author declares upon oath
That his life has been modelled upon both.

Written by Bentley on the front free endpaper of a copy of the
first edition of *Biography for Beginners*

Introduction

GAVIN EWART

EDMUND CLERIHEW BENTLEY, famous as the inventor of the clerihew and (to a lesser extent) as the author of the detective story *Trent's Last Case*, was born in London in 1875 and died there in 1956. He was for more than twenty years chief leader-writer on the *Daily Telegraph*. There is quite a long entry concerning him in the *Dictionary of National Biography 1951–1960* and a shorter one, enjoyable for those who appreciate telegraphese, in *Who Was Who 1951–1960*:

BENTLEY, EDMUND CLERIHEW; Writer; *b.* 10 July 1875; *e.s.* of late J. E. Bentley and M. R. Clerihew; *m.* 1902, Violet (*d.* 1949), *d.* of Gen. N. E. Boileau, Bengal Staff Corps; two *s. Educ.:* St. Paul's School; Merton College, Oxford (scholar, B.A.). President Oxford Union Society, 1898; called to Bar, Inner Temple, 1901; joined staff of Daily News in 1902; leader-writer on Daily Telegraph, 1912–34; rejoined staff 1940; writer of detective novels and short stories since 1912; contributor of prose and verse to many periodicals since 1896. *Publications:* Biography For Beginners, 1905; Trent's Last Case, 1912; More Biography, 1929; Trent's Own Case (with H. Warner Allen), 1936; Trent Intervenes, 1938; Baseless Biography, 1939; Those Days, 1940; Elephant's Work, 1950; Clerihews Complete, 1951.

This has the main facts of his life (though he had one daughter who died as a child and *Clerihews Complete* wasn't complete). His own autobiography *Those Days* and his son Nicolas Bentley's *A Version Of The Truth* (1960) are the two important source books. The latter tells us a good deal about him, giving life to the bare bones in *Who Was Who*. The son's-eye view is often a clear one.

His father, according to Nicolas, 'was extraordinarily reserved'. 'He was cultivated and widely read, but in most matters of taste he was a Philistine', 'always a stickler for physical fitness', but 'gradually he degenerated into a hopeless hypochondriac, and later on in life he began to hit the bottle'. The cause of this, Nicolas thought, was his failure to get the First in Greats that he expected and to make his mark in the world as his Oxford contemporaries did (Lord Birkenhead, John Buchan).

Nicolas writes: 'I don't remember his ever listening to the radio of his own accord.' Even when bedridden he 'could not be persuaded to look at television'; 'his interest in contemporary literature, particularly fiction, was extraordinarily meagre'. In the latter part of his life he never went to theatres, cinemas or concerts. Nicolas concludes: 'I think it gave him more pleasure than anything else he achieved in life that he lived to see the word "clerihew" . . . enshrined in the Oxford Dictionary as part of our language.'

Bentley's wife, according to Nicolas, suffered from too great a sense of 'family' and was ridiculously proud of being descended from the great French poet Boileau. She called H. G. Wells 'a common little man'. On the other hand, her father, though a General, was charming, intelligent, a radical, a crank and a free thinker; very much in the mould of Anthony Powell's General Conyers, one might think. Thus are the expectations aroused by condensed biography defeated.

Bentley was an intelligent gent – and by this I mean a well-educated member of the English upper classes – liberal and uncensorious in his instincts, a member of the Fabian Society at Oxford (but also an enthusiastic rowing man), born when income tax stood at 2d. in the pound and the British Empire looked as though it would last for ever. But Bentley was very far from being a reactionary jingoist. In his autobiography he wrote, of the Nazis in the 1930s, that they 'pretended, for fear of violence, to believe in a body of pseudo-scientific racial rubbish that is beneath the contempt of every disciplined mind'. At this time there were many Conservatives who regarded the Hitler regime with favour.

In *Trent's Last Case*, published in 1912, the most unpleasant character by a very long way is the murderee Sigsbee Manderson, financier and millionaire capitalist. Julian Symons has pointed out that the detective story writers in the so-called 'Golden Age' of the twenties (Dorothy Sayers, Agatha Christie and Anthony Berkeley in Britain) 'would not have held it against Manderson that he had become rich by speculation'. This social radicalism was inspired by Bentley's old school friend G. K. Chesterton, to whom the book was dedicated. Chesterton later, in 1928, founded the Detection Club, of which he himself was President.

Chesterton was an almost exact contemporary, born one year earlier. When Bentley was twelve he went to St. Paul's, the famous London boys' school, where he met Chesterton for the first time. It was here in 1890, when he was sixteen (so he remembers), that Bentley wrote the first clerihew. In *Those Days* it reads:

> Sir Humphry Davy
> Detested gravy.
> He lived in the odium
> Of having discovered Sodium.

(The version published in 1905 reads 'Abominated'.) This was illustrated by Chesterton, and the collaboration produced many more. It's interesting that this very first clerihew was never bettered by Bentley. Like a lot of young people's poetry it seemed to come out of the blue, according to Bentley's account. Chesterton wrote clerihews as well (though not one of them is preserved in his *Collected Poems*), and later pursued his draughtsmanship at the Slade School. They remained close friends for the rest of their lives.

Bentley's account of all this in *Those Days* isn't entirely accurate. It seems that he was probably nearer eighteen than sixteen when he immortalized Sir Humphry Davy, and a notebook is in existence (now in the Library of St. Paul's School) which contains the first clerihews collected together.[1] This is dated September 1893, when Bentley would have been eighteen. There are 132 of them, all but the introductory clerihew illustrated by Chesterton, written by Bentley and his Pauline friends and also by Chesterton's father. The author of each clerihew has a pictorial symbol, drawn as part of the illustration by Chesterton (Bentley is a dodo, for example) alongside the verse, so assigning authorship isn't difficult. Where there was collaboration, more than one symbol appears. The verses are in Bentley's handwriting. Besides Bentley himself, who wrote most of them, the list of contributors reads: G. K. Chesterton, L. R. F. Oldershaw, Edward Chesterton, W. P. H. d'Avigdor, Maurice Solomon. In fact, the notebook was a present to Solomon from Bentley, and it was later presented to St. Paul's by Solomon's widow. Of the 132 notebook clerihews only 21 were ever published in books – and six of these in altered versions. Davy's verse, the great prototype, claimed only that he 'Was not fond of' gravy. The notebook reveals that some of the clerihews Bentley later published (surely inadvertently) as his own were in fact written by or in collaboration with his friends, or at any rate recognizably derived from such originals.

First written for fun, as a relaxation from school work, Bentley's clerihews were not published until fifteen years later, in 1905, under the pseudonym of E. Clerihew (his mother's maiden name and his own second name). Bentley wrote, in *Those Days*, that they 'had never a popular success'; he also wrote: 'I never heard who started the practice of referring to this literary form – if that is the word – as a Clerihew; but it began early, and the name stuck.' Clerihews were written, apparently, by James Elroy Flecker and by Charles Scott-Moncrieff. Like the lost plays of Euripides, these seem to have vanished.

[1] See E. Clerihew Bentley and others, *The First Clerihews* (Oxford University Press, 1982), an interleaved facsimile edition of this valuable work.

At Oxford in the nineties Bentley was fond of P. G. Wodehouse, critical of the hard-drinking lobster-eating non-reading *jeunesse dorée*, but not an 'aesthete'. He was never, I suppose, an extremist. Although he admired Chesterton and Hilaire Belloc – and the latter's best poetry, the *Cautionary Tales*, is light verse of the highest kind – Bentley was not a Catholic. Nor, like them, a Catholic apologist. One clerihew suggests that Bunyan's *Pilgrim's Progress* might be lent to a wicked ogress, and Chesterton's illustration shows the book being posted into a mouth like an enormous letter box. Another concerns Mr. Alfred Beit, who 'screamed suddenly in the night'; no reason is given. Chesterton's picture, however, where Beit is in bed surrounded by moneybags, makes it fairly clear that he is a German–Jewish financier (meerschaum pipe, china tankard, German arms on the wall). The inference is that it was consciousness of the sin of usury that caused him to scream. Bernard Shaw is depicted as a coward, perhaps for his pro-Boer pronouncements:

> Mr. Bernard Shaw
> Was just setting out for the war,
> When he heard it was a dangerous trade
> And demonstrably underpaid.

but this is surprising in a way, since Bentley and his friends regarded the Boer War as a capitalist adventure, with the South African diamond mines as the prize. In the clerihews Karl Marx is treated with humour, not disapproval. The Primrose League is referred to, obliquely, as an 'unburied ichthyosaurus'. Henry Ford (another millionaire) is satirised for meanness. Political figures such as Snowden, Ramsay MacDonald and Maxton, and American Presidents like Coolidge and Hoover, are not directly criticised for their activities or beliefs. It is all very mild. Even Hitler (*Baseless Biography* was published in 1939) is treated facetiously in the clerihew devoted to Goering:

'The moustache of Adolf Hitler
Could hardly be littler,'
Was the thought that kept recurring
To Field Marshal Goering.

This is mild indeed, considering what Bentley thought of the
Nazis. He considered them crude, cruel and bad-mannered
compared to the imperialistic militarists of the Kaiser's time, who
at least were gentlemen, though of an arrogant and unpleasant
sort. Bentley spent a lot of time, as a young man, walking through
Europe. He saw the admired German Army at close quarters on
manoeuvres and witnessed the worship accorded to it by the
civilian population in the years immediately before 1914.

The classical clerihew, then, is free from malice. Bentley
probably thought that Beit was a villain, but he doesn't say so.
The illustration is far more outspoken; Chesterton was a great
arguer and far more of a polemicist. The clerihew could easily be
used for satire, and even satire of great bitterness, but as far as I
know it never has been. The element of absurdity was there from
the first (Sir Humphry Davy), along with the challenge of names
that were hard to rhyme, and it belongs to the clerihew – just as
jollity, scurrility and sexiness belong to the classical limerick. It's
mainly a question of tone, and the tone of the clerihew is both
civilised and dotty.

On page 79 of Frances Stillman's extremely comprehensive and
useful transatlantic work of reference, *The Poet's Manual and
Rhyming Dictionary* (1966), there is the following definition of the
clerihew:

The clerihew is named in honor of its inventor, Edmund Clerihew
Bentley. It is a humorous pseudo-biographical quatrain, rhymed as
two couplets, with lines of uneven length more or less in the
rhythm of prose. It is short and pithy, and often contains or implies
a moral reflection of some kind. The name of the individual who is
the subject of the quatrain usually supplies the first line.

LOUIS XVI

The Sixteenth Louis
Exclaimed, 'Phooey!'
Then, 'Heavens! What was that I said?
I must have lost my head.'

F.S.

This is a sound definition, except that the 'moral reflection' is often entirely absent in Bentley's pieces. Ms. Stillman's own example makes clear another interesting fact about the form. Nobody much except Bentley has ever written really good clerihews. Even W. H. Auden's *Academic Graffiti* are not satisfactory; in fact they are the least effective poems he wrote.

My First Name, *Wystan*,
Rhymes with *Tristan*,
But – O dear! – I do hope
I'm not quite such a dope.

This is sad stuff for a major poet. A few are up to the highest Bentley standards, but not many. Two of the best are on Blake and Clough:

William Blake
Found Newton hard to take,
And was not enormously taken
With Francis Bacon.

When Arthur Hugh Clough
Was jilted by a piece of fluff,
He sighed 'Quel dommage!',
And wrote *Amours de Voyage*.

Anachronism is at the heart of a good many of Bentley's, and Auden has this too; Thackeray is rhymed with daiquiri, for example.

Although the word 'clerihew' has passed into the language, it would still be only a fairly literary kind of person who would know what the word meant. Until quite recently, even in the best dictionaries, there was no entry between 'clerify' and 'clerisy'. Definitions of the word 'limerick', on the other hand and naturally enough, have been offered for a long time.

From the very beginning, even in their early days, clerihews were known to the literate; and now, particularly to the editors of anthologies of light verse, the form is a well-known one. In the American William Cole's *The Fireside Book of Humorous Poetry* (1959) – to give only one example – there is a section entitled 'The Soul of Wit', described as 'an omnium-gatherum of clerihews, epigrams and other pithy pieces'. One can see at once (as the mammoth is the ancestor of the modern elephant) how Blake's epigram on Sir Joshua Reynolds is the true ancestor of the clerihew:

> When Sir Joshua Reynolds died
> All Nature was degraded;
> The King dropped a tear into the Queen's ear,
> And all his pictures faded.

This has the right element of fantasy, though it is not mild. Blake means what he says – or implies – that Reynolds was a successful fraud. The metre, though, has something in common with that of the limerick. It is still a rhyming epigram and not a clerihew.

Among the true clerihews that Cole includes (and the majority are the famous ones by Bentley) there are some that reach the required standard:

JACOBEAN

Henry James
(Whatever his other claims)
Is not always too deuced
Lucid.

This is Clifton Fadiman (American).

> Massenet
> Never wrote a Mass in A.
> It'd have been just too bad,
> If he had.

This is by Antony Butts (British). Allan M. Laing has a very Bentleian touch:

> Samuel Pepys
> said it gave him the creeps
> to see Nell Gwynn beckoned
> by Charles the Second.

and there is a good one by an anonymous writer ('Lakon'):

> William the Bastard
> Frequently got plastered
> In a manner unbecoming to the successor
> Of Edward the Confessor.

Ogden Nash, the best modern writer of trivia, never wrote an actual clerihew, though at least one of his epigrammatic comments is very near to one:

> THE CANARY
>
> The song of canaries
> Never varies
> And when they're moulting
> They're pretty revolting.

The best non-Bentley work in the genre is by Maurice Hare:

> BYWAYS IN BIOGRAPHY
>
> Alfred de Musset
> Used to call his cat Pusset.
> His accent was affected.
> That was to be expected.

Another book that contains very good examples is a rare publication of 1938, *Clerihews*, edited by John Waynflete Carter, printed at the Rampant Lion Press in Cambridge. This describes itself as 'An unofficial supplement to "Biography For Beginners"' and the dedication reads:

> In the belief that imitation is still the sincerest
> form of flattery, this little anthology is dedicated,
> with the diffidence born of admiration,
> TO THE MASTER

There is a fine one by Bentley's son Nicolas (his last illustrator):

> Cecil B. de Mille,
> Rather against his will,
> Was persuaded to leave Moses
> Out of 'The Wars of the Roses'.

Other good ones are by E. W. Fordham:

> Miss Mae West
> Is one of the best:
> I would rather not
> Say the best what.

by John Sparrow:

> Sir Lancelot
> Used to dance a lot.
> None of the dancers
> Could beat him at The Lancers.

and by Constant Lambert:

> 'Anthony Adverse'
> May not be bad verse.
> But God knows
> It's bad prose.

There is even what Carter calls 'a discarded child of Mr. E. C. Bentley himself':

> Louis Quatorze
> Had a penchant for wars.
> He sent Turenne to the Palatinate
> With instructions to flatten it.

This comes from an article contributed by Bentley in 1930 to the *Week-end Review* (and reprinted in *Those Days*), in which he undertakes a mock-serious analysis of the literary form he invented. He criticizes the clerihew above for its lack of fantasy, and also disparages:

> Frederick the Great
> Became King at twenty-eight.
> In a fit of amnesia
> He invaded Silesia.

though the first seems to me quite as good as the best he allowed into his canon. Another eventual throw-out, on Julius Caesar (see overleaf), did appear in *Punch* in 1938, as part of a series of clerihews that were then included in *Baseless Biography*. That's how it acquired the Nicolas Bentley illustration reproduced with it. But Bentley evidently had second thoughts about it, since it didn't end up in the book. It is the only 'mono-rhymed' clerihew he published.

I was surprised that Carter's modest and beautifully printed little book has a 'cupboard' number in the British Library Catalogue – in other words, it's in with the obscene books. Was Mae West's reputation thought to be in danger in 1938? Italians are referred to in one clerihew as 'wops', there is an uncomplimentary piece about Goering, while another reads:

> The Mikado of Japan
> Is a most extraordinary man.
> He lives in the tops of trees
> Surrounded by Japanese.

Caius Julius Caesar
Patented a lemon-squeezer,
Also an ice-cream freezer
And a chariot axle-greaser.

It appears, however, that modesty, libel and political expediency were not at stake. Private press books have 'cupboard' numbers too.

Clerihews go on being written. A recent Oxonian anonymity, printed in *The Pelican 1978–79*, has the true Bentley touch:

> Q. Horatius Flaccus
> Wrote an Ode about Bacchus,
> But Bacchus was far too shy
> To write a reply.

I have myself written clerihews, none of which has made me feel particularly proud; this is a recent one:

> Clio
> wasn't happy in Ohio
> and V. Sackville-West and Violet Trefusis
> were more congenial to her than the other eight Muses.

In December 1980 the Weekend Competition in the *New Statesman* invited clerihews on existing newspapers and magazines; and in 1981 the *Sunday Times* ran a clerihew competition. Bentley's work is a perpetual challenge. Good clerihews have been written since his day; but the inspired lighthearted silliness and unlikeliness of the originals are not easily come by.

GAVIN EWART

Note on the Revised Edition

A REVISED edition of a book claiming completeness is
an odd enough idea to warrant a word of explanation.
The discovery of the school notebook in which Bentley
wrote the first clerihews composed by himself and his
friends as teenagers required an adjustment to Gavin
Ewart's introduction. Two new 'throw-out' clerihews
and two further Nicolas Bentley illustrations came to
light and have been added (pp. xx and xxiv). The 'Pre-
face to the New Edition' written by Bentley for the third
edition (1925) of *Biography for Beginners* now fits (with
minimal tinkering) the present context. Several textual
emendations have been introduced after diligent com-
parison of different versions of the clerihews published by
Bentley. These include the restoration of some authorial
footnotes present only in the first edition of *Biography
for Beginners*. (Shortage of space has prevented one of
these appearing *in situ*. In the clerihew on Davy (p. 38),
'Sodium' was originally annotated thus: 'This widely-
diffused and abundant element was, in a sense, dis-
covered in 1736 by Duhamel, who first recognized it as
a distinct substance; but it was first obtained in the
metallic state by Davy in 1807.') The index has been
greatly enlarged to include all the entries from the origi-
nal indexes, not just a selection as before. The few
further changes are trivial by comparison.

P.S. At the last minute an unpublished autobio-
graphical clerihew turned up. It has been slipped in on
p. viii.

Note on the Illustrations

ILLUSTRATIONS which originally appeared in *More Biography* (1929) bear their artists' initials (NB, ECB, GKC or VR). G. K. Chesterton drew the illustrations to the subjects of *Biography for Beginners* (1905) (Introductory Remarks, Austen, Beit, Belloc, Besant and Rice, Bunyan, Cervantes, Chapman & Hall, Cimabue, Clifford, Clive, Davy, Dewar, Edward the Confessor, Erasmus, Fife, Fuller Acland-Hood, Grieg, Harley, Hirst, Hume, Job, Liszt, Mahomet, Malory, Marconi, Marx, Mill, Odo, Otto, Pizarro, Raleigh, Ricardo, Roosevelt, Shaw, Tiziano, Van Eyck, Wellington, Werner Laurie and Wren) and the frontispiece (p. ii), which originally appeared on the front cover of the first edition of that book (a caricature of Bentley often appears in Chesterton's pictures, usually when the text refers to the author in the first person). All others, first collectively published as *Baseless Biography* (1939) – some had previously appeared in *Punch* – are by the author's son, Nicolas Bentley, who also drew Caesar (see p. xx) and the jacket illustration for *More Biography* reproduced overleaf.

To have enriched and refined
The universal mind
Affords me some measure
Of not ignoble pleasure.

Author's Preface

I am unable to withstand
The world-wide demand
For another edition
Of this work of exposition.

I can no longer close my ears
To the entreaties and tears,
The passionate supplications,
Of the yearning nations.

To have enriched and refined
The universal mind
Affords me some measure
Of not ignoble pleasure.

But what most touches my heart
Is the contemplation of the part
Played by this that I have written
In the intellectual life of Britain.

To the biographic art
It has been able to impart
What is described by Dr. Limpet as
A new and salutary impetus.

On biographic style
(Formerly so vile)
My work has had an effect
Greater than I could reasonably expect.

The spirit and method
Have been immeasurably bettered,
And biography day by day
Has improved in every way.

I might instance Sir Sidney Lee's
Sympathetic handling of cheese,
Or Mr. G. M. Trevelyan's
Patient way with Italians;

While it would be an unpardonable laches
To deny to Mr. Lytton Strachey's
Masterly treatment of Vespasian
A word of hearty commendation.

*　　*　　*

If I may glance briefly at a
Purely personal matter,
I would refer to a change on that vital page
Technically known as the title-page.

When first it dawned upon mankind,
Biography for Beginners was signed
(For reasons with which I will not weary you)
With the name of E. Clerihew.

I am not without a claim
To the use of that honourable name,
Which those who happened to be listening
Heard bestowed on me at my christening.

But (for reasons which would only bore you)
The name on the collection before you
Has been changed—I hope not detrimentally—
To E. Clerihew Bentley.

Introductory Remarks

The Art of Biography
Is different from Geography.
Geography is about Maps,
But Biography is about Chaps.

'Steady the Greeks!' shouted Aeschylus.
'We won't let such dogs as these kill us!'
Nothing, he thought, could be bizarrer than
The Persians winning at Marathon.

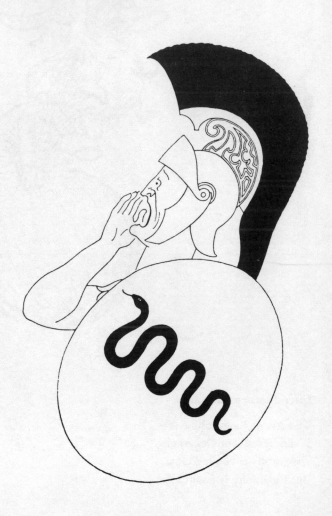

Alexander of Macedon
Became gloomy and taciturn
When they told him at the 'Blue Lion'
That he couldn't have any more Chian.

When a photograph of Attila
Appeared in the *Tatler*
The Huns were all delighted,
And the editor was knighted.

The novels of Jane Austen
Are the ones to get lost in.
I wonder if Labby*
Has read *Northanger Abbey*?

* See Index (ed.).

When their lordships asked Bacon
How many bribes he had taken
He had at least the grace
To get very red in the face.

When the Venerable Bede
Wanted to play Juvenile Lead*
They said they would much rather
He took the Heavy Father.

* 'Cur non ? Quid si prisca redit venus ?'
Epistola ad Ecgbertum, §127.

Mr. Alfred Beit
Screamed suddenly in the night.
When they asked him why
He made no reply.

Mr. Hilaire Belloc
Is a case for legislation *ad hoc.*
He seems to think nobody minds
His books being all of different kinds.

Sir (then Mr.) Walter Besant
Would never touch pheasant,
But Mr. James Rice
Thought it *so* nice.

'Corruptio optimi pessima!'
Grinned Sir Henry Bessemer.
'Judicio vulgi demens!'
Snorted Sir William Siemens.

'Sire!' exclaimed Bossuet,
'You are behaving in a gross way.'
'Still, it's rather a lark,'
Replied the Grand Monarque.

Although Don Bradman
Screamed and fought like a madman
And condemned the proceedings *in toto*,
They insisted on taking his photo.

It only irritated Brahms
To tickle him under the arms.
What really helped him to compose
Was to be stroked on the nose.

When Macaulay found Brougham
Sitting on a tomb,
He told an anxious friend
He was meditating on his latter end.

On one occasion when Browning
Saved a débutante from drowning
She inquired faintly what he meant
By that stuff about good news from Ghent.

I do not extenuate Bunyan's
Intemperate use of onions,
But if I knew a wicked ogress
I would* lend her *The Pilgrim's Progress*.

* 'Should' may, if preferred, be used here.

Sir Edward Burne-Jones
Was usually Mistah Bones
And imitated a German taking soup
In the Pre-Raphaelite Minstrel Troupe.

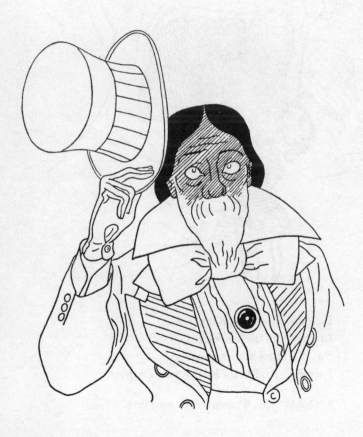

'Gentlemen,' said Burns,
'Before the meeting adjourns
I think the least we can do
Is to declare that we are nae fou.'

I fear that King Canute
Was rather a secretive sort of brute.
He would never admit it, but
His name was really Knut.

Thomas Carlyle
Suffered with his bile.
He wrote *Sartor Resartus*;
But that shan't part us.

Lewis Carroll
Bought sumptuous apparel
And built an enormous palace
Out of the profits of *Alice*.

That time when Lord Cecil
Induced Sir Austin to wrestle
Delegates rushed up in a fever
From all over Geneva.

The people of Spain think Cervantes
Equal to half a dozen Dantes:
An opinion resented most bitterly
By the people of Italy.

Chapman & Hall
Swore not at all.
Mr. Chapman's yea was yea,
And Mr. Hall's nay was nay.

Geoffrey Chaucer
Took a bath (in a saucer)
In consequence of certain hints
Dropped by the Black Prince.

When they told Cimabue
He didn't know how to cooee,
He replied, 'Perhaps I mayn't,
But I do know how to paint.'

The one thing Cleopatra
Never could abide was a flatterer.
When Antony compared her to Thaïs
She knocked him right off the dais.

Dr. Clifford
And I have differed.
He disapproves of gin:
I disapprove of sin.

What I like about Clive
Is that he is no longer alive.
There is a great deal to be said
For being dead.

'I quite realized', said Columbus,
'That the Earth was not a rhombus,
But I *am* a little annoyed
To find it an oblate spheroid.'

The only occasion when Comte
Is known to have romped
Was when the multitude roared, 'Vive
La Philosophie Positive!'

President Coolidge
Objected to paying muleage
When the people of Nicaragua
Sent him a nice jaguar.

One day the putting of Cotton
Was so indescribably rotten
That H.H. the Sultan of Johore
Beat him by 6 and 4.

Mr. Noel Coward
Was disillusioned and soured
By the lukewarm reception of his comedy
Introducing a real dromedary.*

* Named Ethel.

What if Bishop Creighton
Was descended from a Titan?
A man I know called Binks
Is descended from the Sphinx.

Dante Alighieri
Seldom troubled a dairy.
He wrote the *Inferno*
On a bottle of Pernod.

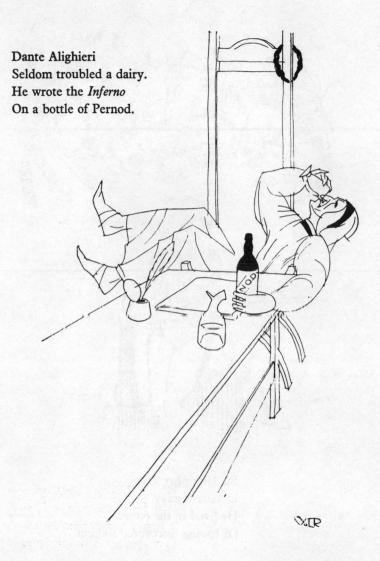

Sir Humphry Davy
Detested gravy.
He lived in the odium
Of having discovered sodium.

Professor Dewar
Is a better man than you are.
None of you asses
Can condense gases.

It was a pity about Dickens'
Insane jealousy of chickens,
And one could really almost weep
At his morbid mistrust of sheep.

A man in the position
Of the Emperor Domitian
Ought to have thought twice
About being a Monster of Vice.

Edward the Confessor
Slept under the dresser.
When that began to pall,
He slept in the hall.

After dinner, Erasmus
Told Colet not to be 'blas'mous',
Which Colet, with some heat,
Challenged him to repeat.

It looked bad when the Duke of Fife
Left off using a knife;
But people began to talk
When he left off using a fork.

Mr. Henry Ford
Had a little secret hoard,
To which he would add a dime
From time to time.

'Give me', sang Mr. Fox,
'To wanton with thy locks.'
'That I will never permit!'
Exclaimed Mr. Pitt.

Sir Alexander Acland-Hood
Believed in Free Food;
But he was Eleusinian
About this opinion.

Sir Alexander Fuller Acland-Hood, MP 47

The meaning of the poet Gay
Was always as clear as day,
While that of the poet Blake
Was often practically opaque.

George the Third
Ought never to have occurred.
One can only wonder
At so grotesque a blunder.

'The moustache of Adolf Hitler
Could hardly be littler,'
Was the thought that kept recurring
To Field Marshal Goering.

Dr. W. G. Grace
Had hair all over his face.
Lord! how the people cheered
When a ball got lost in his beard!

No doubt the poet Gray
Was all very well in his way,
But he couldn't write a song
Like 'Now We Shan't Be Long'.

The musician Grieg
Joined the Primrose League.
It gave him the idea of his chorus,
'The Unburied Ichthyosaurus'.

It is curious that Handel
Should always have used a candle.
Men of his stamp
Generally use a lamp.

It was rather disconcerting for Hannibal
To be introduced to a cannibal
Who expressed the very highest opinion
Of cold pickled Carthaginian.

People wondered why Harley
Sang 'Wae's me for Prince Charlie'.
'It is childish', they said, 'to mourn
For a person not yet born.'

Henry the First
Ate lampreys till he burst;
His unfortunate decease
Simply ruined the Norman peace.

Henry the Eighth
Took a thuctheththion of mateth.
He inthithted that the monkth
Were a lathy lot of thkunkth.

Inspiration visited Herrick
During a mixed foursome at North Berwick.
When his partner had sliced into a drain
He wrote 'To Anthea, Who Gives Him a
    Pain'.

When I faced the bowling of Hirst
I ejaculated, 'Do your worst!'
He said, 'Right you are, Sid.'
—And he did.

'Dear me!' exclaimed Homer,
'What a delicious aroma!
It smells as if a town
Was being burnt down.'

President Hoover
Felt in need of a soother
After his little tiff
With Governor Al Smith.

'How many times', mused Hugo,
'Do fours into 372 go?
Come, now; let me see.
I have it—*Ninety-three !*'

That you have all heard of Hume
I tacitly assume;
But you didn't know, perhaps,
That his parents were Lapps.

'Susaddah!' exclaimed Ibsen,
'By dose is turdig cribson!
I'd better dot kiss you.
Atishoo! Atishoo!'

It maddened Dean Inge
To be asked not to sing,*
And there was some savage biting
When they tried to stop him reciting.†

* 'The Gipsy's Warning'.
† 'Zara's Ear-rings'.

Sir James Jeans
Always says what he means;
He is really perfectly serious
About the Universe being Mysterious.

It is understood that Job
Never read the *Globe*;
But nothing could be higher than
His opinion of Leviathan.

I doubt if King John
Was a *sine qua non*.
I could rather imagine it
Of any other Plantagenet.

How the Emperor Jovian
Would have revelled in the *Harrovian*!
And can't you see Diocletian
Roaring over the *Fettesian*?

Sir William Joynson-Hicks
Could only count up to six,
Which was rather a wrecker
For his hopes of the Exchequer.*

* Sir William received in 1929 the
consolation of a Peerage of the
United Kingdom under the name,
style and title of Viscount Brentford,
of Newick in the County of Sussex.

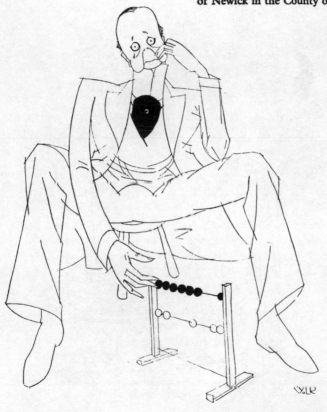

John Keats
Among other notable feats
Drank off a soup-tureen
Full of the true, the blushful Hippocrene.

It was useless to tell a man
So opinionated as Kellerman
That he was absolutely balmy
To think of standing at Valmy.

Dame Laura Knight
Had unusually keen sight.
She could spot a circus clown, they say,
A couple of miles away.

The sermons of John Knox
Teemed with disapproval of frocks.
There was no acquiescence by him in
The Monstrous Regiment of Women.

Archbishop Laud
Saw nothing to admire in *Maud*.
The line he thought most appalling
Was 'Little King Charles is snarling.'

It was a rule of Leonardo da Vinci's
Not to put his trust in princes.
Pleading was of no avail;
They had to pay up on the nail.

The Abbé Liszt
Hit the piano with his fist.
That was the way
He used to play.

François Liszt

Louis the Eleventh
Was contemporary with Henry the Seventh.
I am glad that he
Was not contemporary with me.

Louis Dixhuit
Got decidedly cold feet
When he heard that the Little Man
Had landed at Cannes.

Mr. Ramsay MacDonald
Wished the Channel could be tunnelled.
He said it always got his goat
To be asked if he had lunched on the boat.

Although Machiavelli
Was extremely fond of jelly,
He stuck religiously to mince
While he was writing *The Prince*.

I am *not* Mahomet.*
—Far from it.
That is the mistake
All of you seem to make.

* 'More properly Mohammed'.
Gibbon, *Decline and Fall of the
Roman Empire*, chap. 1.

Sir Thomas à Malory
Always went to the gallery.
He said, not without nous,
That it was the best place in the house.

Guglielmo Marconi
Was brought up on macaroni,
But when he gets it now
There's no end of a row.

The Empress Maria Theresa
Had a poodle called Sneezer
Which severely bit
A Prussian from Tilsit.

Karl Marx
Was completely wrapped up in his sharks.
The poor creatures seriously missed him
While he was attacking the capitalist system.

As a laddie, Mrr. Maxton
Was apprrenticed tae a saxton.
He thot it wid be prime
To hae Socialism in oor time.

In later life Methuselah
Became a hopeless foozler.
After he was 765
He practically never hit a decent drive.

John Stuart Mill,
By a mighty effort of will,
Overcame his natural bonhomie
And wrote *Principles of Political Economy*.*

* '—*With some of their Applications to Social
Philosophy*'.

The digestion of Milton
Was unequal to stilton.
He was only feeling so-so
When he wrote 'Il Penseroso'.

Signor Mussolini
Disliked the name Sweeney.
Anyone bearing it, he said,
Would get a clump on the head.

'Ow!' screamed Beverley Nichols.
'Take it away! It tickles!
You *know* I simply can't bear
An earwig loose in my hair.'

Archbishop Odo
Was just in the middle of *Dodo*,
When he remembered that it was Sunday.
Sic transit gloria mundi.

The great Emperor Otto
Could not decide upon a motto.
His mind wavered between
L'État c'est moi and *Ich dien*.

'No,' said Charles Peace,
'I can't 'ardly blame the perlice.
They 'as their faults, it is true,
But I sees their point of view.'

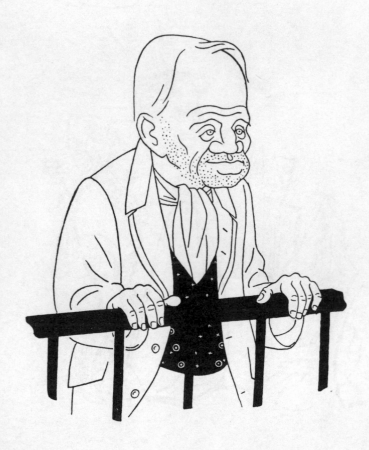

Sir Robert Peel
Said it was not genteel
But, on the contrary, very rude
To tax the people's food.

Peter the Hermit
Neglected to apply for a permit
When raising his mixed brigade
For the First Crusade.

Few Romans were as tony as
The elegant Petronius.
None who dressed snappier
Appeared on the Via Appia.

The views of Pizarro
Were perhaps a little narrow.
He killed the Caciques
Because (he said) they were sneaks.

Although the dialogues of Plato
Do not actually mention the potato,
They inculcate strongly we should
Seek the Absolute Ideal Good.

Edgar Allan Poe
Was passionately fond of roe.
He always liked to chew some
When writing anything gruesome.

'Tiens!' fit M. Poincaré,
'On annonce vingt minutes d'arrêt!
Un coup de vin, qu'il est bon!
Allons! Garçon!'

When Alexander Pope
Accidentally trod on the soap
And came down on the back of his head—
Never mind what he said.

Sir Walter Raleigh
Bickered down the valley.
But he could do better than the rill,
For he could bicker uphill.

Of course Ranjitsinhji
Was quite right not to be stingy,
But I never could quite see the relevance
Of his keeping nine thousand elephants.

The intrepid Ricardo,
With characteristic bravado,
Alluded openly to Rent
Wherever he went.

If only Mr. Roosevelt
Knew how officers in the Blues felt,
He wouldn't be so rife
With his Strenuous Life.

The poems of Rossetti
Were sweetly pretty,
Especially that one which began,
'Why did you melt your waxen man?'

Rupert of the Rhine
Thought Cromwell was a swine,
And he felt quite sure
After Marston Moor.

Savonarola
Declined to wear a bowler,
Expressing the view that it was gammon
To talk of serving God and Mammon.

Miss Dorothy Sayers
Never cared about the Himalayas.
The height that gave her a thrill
Was Primrose Hill.

I believe it was admitted by Scott
That some of his novels were rot.
How different was he from Lytton,
Who admired everything he had written!

Among the contemporaries of Shakespeare
There were few who regarded him as Drake's peer.
Spoiling paper was so much less strain
Than spoiling the Spanish Main.

Mr. Bernard Shaw
Was just setting out for the war,
When he heard it was a dangerous trade
And demonstrably underpaid.

'No, sir,' said General Sherman,
'I did *not* enjoy the sermon;
Nor I didn't git any
Kick outer the Litany.'

True, Lambert Simnel
Was not an habitual criminal,
But it really was hardly historic
To call himself Earl of Warwick.

Adam Smith
Was disowned by all his kith,
But he was backed through thick and thin
By all his kin.

Mr. Philip Snowden
Was rarely mistaken for Woden.
People as a rule were much more
Apt to mistake him for Thor.

How vigilant was Spenser
As a literary censor!
He pointed out that there were too few E's
In Lyly's *Euphues*.

Bishop Stubbs
Was expelled from all his clubs
For disparaging the Oxford crew
In the *Quarterly Review*.

Somebody sent Dean Swift
An ounce of strychnine as a gift.
He took about thirty-five minims
While writing about the Houyhnhms.

As a young man, Tennyson
Wrote a virelay about venison,
Which falls into the same group
With his *sirvente* about soup.

When the late Titian
Was in a critical condition,
He was carefully nursed
By Francis the First.

When Torquemada
Found a cat in the larder
He relinquished it without a qualm*
To the Secular Arm.

* Although its name was Ferdinand.

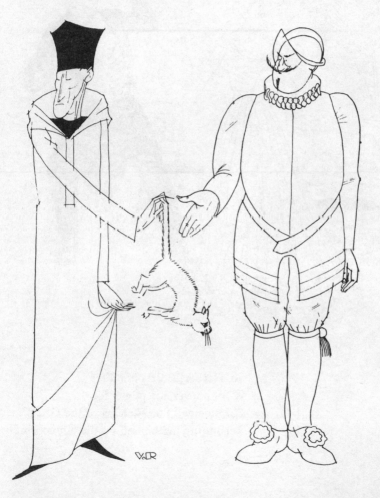

Sir Herbert Beerbohm Tree
Would never accept any fee
For singing 'The Wearing of the Green',
Accompanying himself on the tambourine.

Martin Tupper
Sang for his supper;
Though the supper wasn't nice,
It was cheap at the price.

That sensitive genius Turner
Simply detested Smyrna.
He said, give him Mozambique
Any day in the week.

The younger Van Eyck
Was christened Jan, and not Mike.
The thought of this curious mistake
Often kept him awake.

It was a weakness of Voltaire's
To forget to say his prayers,
And one which to his shame
He never overcame.

The works of Edgar Wallace,
Were the unfailing solace
Of a recent Prime Minister
When things were looking sinister.

Of all sad words of tongue or pen
The saddest are Captain Wedgwood Benn,
Who, waving aloft his gory sabre,
Placed it at the disposal of Labour.

The great Duke of Wellington
Reduced himself to a skellington.
He reached seven stone two,
And then—Waterloo!

Mr. H. G. Wells
Was composed of cells.
He thought the human race
Was a perfect disgrace.

'Dinner-time?' said Gilbert White,
'Yes, yes—certainly—all right.
Just let me finish this note
About the Lesser White-bellied Stoat.'

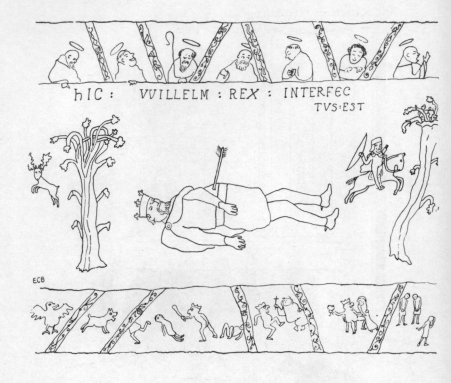

HIC : VVILLELM : REX : INTERFEC
TVS·EST

ECB

There exists no proof as
To who shot William Rufus,
But shooting him would seem*
To have been quite a sound scheme.

* 'Serviit eo hilariter bene recte.'
Will. Malmesb., *Gesta Regum*, lib. xiv, §329.
'Porcus lutulentus id certe poposcit.'
Eadmer, *Hist. Novorum*, lib. ix, p. 34.

Sir Christopher Wren
Said, 'I am going to dine with some men.
If anybody calls
Say I am designing St. Paul's.'

Brigham Young
Was exceptionally highly-strung.
He always used a chopper
When a Mormon said anything improper.

I regard Zinghis Khan
As rather an overrated man.
What, after all, could be easier
Than conquering from the Pacific to
    Silesia?

Mr. Werner Laurie*
Is not at all sorry
He undertook the publication
Of this instructive compilation.

* Publisher of *Biography for
Beginners* (1905) and the so-
called *Clerihews Complete*
(1951) (ed.).

Index of Psychology, Mentality and Other Things

FREQUENTLY NOTED IN CONNECTION
WITH GENIUS

In all work of a biographic character it is important to make copious reference to as many as possible of the generally recognized virtues, vices, good points, foibles, peculiarities, tricks, characteristics, little weaknesses, traits, imperfections, fads, idiosyncrasies, singularities, morbid symptoms, oddities, faults, and regrettable propensities set forth in the following table. The form of an alphabetic index, with references to the examples given in the preceding pages, has been chosen, so that the beginner who may be desirous, when trying his hand at work of this sort, of seeing how any given one of these subjects may best be treated, is enabled at once to turn to one or more model passages.

absurdity (GEORGE III)
accidence (PEACE, SHERMAN)
accidents (GRACE, HENRY I, POPE)
achievement, zenith of literary,
    attainment of (AUSTEN)
Achilles, heel of (JOYNSON-HICKS)
action, prompt and decisive,
    unfitness for position requiring
    (OTTO)
Aesir, confusing resemblance to
    (SNOWDEN)
aggravatingness (BESSEMER, WHITE)
agitation, reluctance to explain
    (BEIT)
Allah, Prophet of, refusal to admit
    identity with (MAHOMET)
amateurishness (ZINGHIS KHAN)
amnesia (ODO, VOLTAIRE)
ancestry (CREIGHTON)

animals, kindness to (JOB, MARIA
    THERESA, MARX)
annoyance (BRADMAN, NICHOLS)
appearances, disregard of, by
    man of position (MALORY)
arithmetic, mental (HUGO)
art, black (BURNE-JONES);
    commercial (LEONARDO)
asceticism (MACHIAVELLI,
    SAVONAROLA)
Athenaeum Club (STUBBS)
atrocity (WREN)
audibility (POPE)

backwardness (POPE)
bankruptcy, moral (WREN)
barberism, methods of (GOERING,
    GRACE)
bathing, mixed (BROWNING)

deceit, abominable (WREN)
deipnomania (TENNYSON)
dejection, stanzas written in,
  nowhere near Naples (MILTON)
delicacy (YOUNG)
descent, long, temptation to smile
  at claims of (CREIGHTON)
diet, indiscretion in (HENRY I,
  MILTON); morbid delicacy in
  matter of (BESANT, DAVY,
  MARCONI, but cf. BUNYAN)
dilettantism (ZINGHIS KHAN)
disagreement, contentions and,
  love of (BESANT and RICE,
  CLIFFORD, ERASMUS, RALEIGH)
discontent, divine (KNOX, LAUD)
disillusionment (BENN, WELLS)
dither, all of a (LOUIS XVIII)
diversity (GAY (& BLAKE))
*divertissement, agréable, au profit de
  la SDN* (CECIL)
dogs, dangerous (AESCHYLUS,
  LAUD, MARIA THERESA)
domesticity (HENRY VIII, IBSEN)
domestic servants, dishonesty
  among, encouragement of
  (WREN)
done, simply not, repugnance to
  what is (PEEL, STUBBS)
dream, boyhood, fulfilment of
  (ATTILA)
dud (GEORGE III)
dudgeon (HERRICK)
duty, agreeable, performance of
  (RUFUS)

Eccentric Club (STUBBS)
efficiency (CIMABUE, DEWAR, HIRST,
  LISZT)
élan (POINCARÉ)
Elks, Brotherly and Protective
  Order of, unfitness to join
  (DOMITIAN, JOHN, RUFUS);
  eligibility for (BOSSUET,
  BROWNING)

emolument (CARROLL,
  LEONARDO, TUPPER)
engagement (AESCHYLUS, RUPERT)
enjoyment, rational (BURNS,
  JOVIAN)
enterprise (KEATS)
entomology, byways of (NICHOLS)
epsilepsy (SPENSER)
escutcheon, blot on, action
  involving (STUBBS, WREN)
etiquette, slavery to (PEEL)
étourderie (GEORGE III)
extraction, Eohellenic (CREIGHTON)
extremity, coolness in (LOUIS XVIII)
eye, eagle (KNIGHT)

Fabius, Quintus, Maximus,
  strategy of, adapted by modern
  votary (SHAW)
fact, cynical perversion of (WREN)
fads (BURNE-JONES, KNOX, LISZT,
  MARX)
faire, savoir (BENN)
fastidiousness (SHERMAN)
fears, worst, confirmation of
  (RUPERT)
feet, the wild mob's million,
  aspiration to cause disuse of
  (FORD)
figure, anxiety about (WELLINGTON)
figures, head for (HUGO)
fire, divine (BRAHMS, DANTE,
  MILTON, POE)
flair (KELLERMAN)
Folly, Carroll's (CARROLL)
foresight (HARLEY, LAUD)
form, bad (STUBBS); intolerance of
  (PEEL)
frenzy (INGE)
frequency, nuptial (HENRY VIII)
fright (BRADMAN, LOUIS XVIII,
  NICHOLS)
frustration (ALEXANDER, ODO)
fullness (BURNS, DANTE)
fussiness (BOSSUET, COLUMBUS)

gaiters, unfitness to wear (STUBBS)
galactophobia (DANTE)
gametomania (HENRY VIII)
gaucherie (GEORGE III)
generalizations, sweeping,
  dangerous fondness for
  (PIZARRO)
genius, hallmarks of: infinite
  capacity for taking drinks
  (DANTE); intolerance
  (TORQUEMADA); lack of balance
  (DICKENS); liability to be
  neglected (SHAKESPEARE); love
  of bright colours (TURNER);
  moral turpitude (RUFUS);
  peevishness (COLUMBUS);
  singularity (HANDEL); ugliness
  (IBSEN); wrangling (BESSEMER)
gerontocracy, resistance to, in
  early English theatre (BEDE)
glamour, negative reaction to
  (KNOX)
glory, uncertain prospect of
  (VOLTAIRE)
godliness, proximity to (CHAUCER,
  POPE)
gourmandise (HANNIBAL, HENRY I,
  MACHIAVELLI)
Greece, the glory that was,
  association with (CREIGHTON,
  HOMER, PLATO); complete
  indifference to (FORD)
Grundy, Mrs., far-reaching
  influence of (YOUNG)
guile (WREN)

habits, repugnant personal, often
  found in association with fine
  spiritual gifts (BUNYAN)
haemalopia (CLEOPATRA)
hair, connoisseurship in (FOX);
  loss of (INGE); pigmentation
  of, moral significance attaching
  to (RUFUS)
handicap, length of (METHUSELAH)

haviour, melancholy, of the visage
  (IBSEN)
heartache (JOYNSON-HICKS)
Hell-Fire Club (STUBBS)
heredity (CREIGHTON)
honesty, blunt (JEANS, SCOTT,
  SHERMAN)
hope, forlorn, perseverance in
  (BOSSUET)
horizon, restricted mental
  (PIZARRO)
horrid, dislike of anything (PEEL)
horror (ALEXANDER, LAUD)
horticulture, pitfalls of (NICHOLS)
howler (GEORGE III)
hubbub, interminable, power to
  raise (MARCONI)
humidity (DANTE)
hump, the, tendency to get
  (COLUMBUS, SHERMAN, VAN EYCK)
hydrostomatitis (TENNYSON)
hygiene (CHAUCER)
hypocrisy, calculated (WREN)

Ichabod! (STUBBS)
idiopathy (MUSSOLINI)
ignoring, pointed, of literary rivals
  (JOB)
illiberality (COOLIDGE)
imbecility (KNOX)
importance (CREIGHTON)
impropriety, condemnation of
  (PEEL)
inadequacy (GRAY)
indirectness (PLATO)
indiscretion, regrettable
  (GEORGE III)
indispensability, more than
  dubious (JOHN)
inexactitude (SIMNEL)
information, insufficient, proneness
  to act upon (ROOSEVELT, SHAW)
insomnia, freedom from (EDWARD
  THE CONFESSOR); liability to
  (BEIT, VAN EYCK)

integrity, low standard of (WREN)
interruption (GRACE, WHITE)
IOU, uncompromising rejection of (LEONARDO)
iron-play, deplorable (METHUSELAH)
ivory, shortage of, nervousness in regard to (RANJITSINHJI)

Jacquerie, leadership of, unfitness for (PEEL)
jealousy (MARIA THERESA); professional (BESSEMER)
Jesuitical dealing (WREN)
jihad, interest in, disclaimer of (MAHOMET); involvement in, anxiety to avoid (TURNER)
jitters (COTTON, LOUIS XVIII); freedom from (AESCHYLUS)
Joan, relations of Darby with, tendency to reproduce (IBSEN)
Jockey Club (STUBBS)
joke, silly practical (GEORGE III)
jollity (DANTE)
joylessness (COMTE)
Juan, Don, imperfect sympathy with (KNOX)
jubilee, non-attainment of (HENRY I)
jumbago (RANJITSINHJI)
justice, passionate love of (TORQUEMADA)
justification, flimsy, of homicide (PIZARRO)

KCSI, merited attainment of (RANJITSINHJI)
ken, mortal, limitations of (JEANS)
kicking, alive and (SWIFT)
kingcraft (CANUTE)
kings, blood of, partiality to (KELLERMANN)
kink, moral (STUBBS); compendious outfit of ——s (DOMITIAN)
kismet, refusal to bow to (INGE)

Klan, Ku Klux, unpopularity among (SHERMAN)
kleptomania ? (PEACE)
knavery (WREN)
knock, nasty, administration of (BENN, HOOVER, MUSSOLINI); reception of (COWARD, JOYNSON-HICKS, SMITH)

Labouchere, Mr., power to awaken interest in (AUSTEN)
laicity (HENRY VIII)
Lakhs, separation from (RANJITSINHJI)
lampadophobia (HANDEL)
lapse, regrettable (GEORGE III)
Latinity (BEDE, BESSEMER, CARLYLE)
levity, ill-timed (FOX); irresponsible, of Yorkshiremen (HIRST)
lie, bouncing, circulation of (WREN)
life, high (ATTILA); low (PEACE); simple, fondness for the (EDWARD THE CONFESSOR, MALORY); wild (WHITE)
limit, the (STUBBS)
linen, fine, purple and (CARROLL)
links, frequentation of (COTTON, HERRICK, METHUSELAH); missing, similarity to (ATTILA, ZINGHIS KHAN)
lineage (CREIGHTON)
lions, little, descent to level of (INGE)
love, withering exposure of (KNOX)
loyalty (CHAUCER, SMITH)
luck!, hard (ALEXANDER, COTTON, METHUSELAH)

Machiavelli, unholy precepts of, tendency to act upon (WREN)
man, ordinary, treatment of genius at hands of (DAVY, HARLEY)
manducation (POE)

manners, good, inculcation of
(PEEL)
Marathon, battle of (AESCHYLUS);
Hippocrene (KEATS); lamprey
(HENRY I); mince (MACHIAVELLI)
mastication (HENRY I, POE)
MCC (STUBBS)
memory, lapse of (ODO)
mercy, bowels of, non-equipment
with (TORQUEMADA)
metaphor, oriental, distaste for
(CHAPMAN & HALL)
mind, contented blessing of a
(MALORY)
mindedness, absent (ODO); broad
(PEACE); high (SAVONAROLA,
WELLS); narrow (KNOX); pure
(ROSSETTI, YOUNG); strong
(CLEOPATRA)
minstrelsy (BURNE-JONES, FOX)
mirth, heart-easing (JOVIAN)
Mjöllnir, misleading effect of,
when carried by Chancellors of
the Exchequer (SNOWDEN)
moderation (SWIFT)
modesty (BRADMAN, SCOTT)
monogamy, recurrent (HENRY VIII)
monster, green-eyed, obsession by
(DICKENS); of ingratitude
(COOLIDGE)
Mormonism, seamy side of (YOUNG)
mulishness (KELLERMAN)
multiplicity (WALLACE)
mutability (BENN)

nail, tooth and, employment of
(BRADMAN)
Nawanagar, Maharajah Jamsaheb
of, HH Shri Sir Ranjitsinhji
Vibaji, determination to keep
up position of (RANJITSINHJI)
negligence (PETER THE HERMIT)
nemesis (STUBBS, TORQUEMADA)
Nepenthe, yearning for (JOYNSON-
HICKS)

nests, birds in their little,
indifference to example of
(KELLERMAN)
nettled, disposition to be easily
(COLUMBUS, INGE, WELLS)
neurosis (YOUNG)
nobility (CREIGHTON)
'noblesse oblige', disregard of
apophthegm (WREN)
norm, departure from the
(HANDEL)
nostrils, free functioning of,
dependence upon (HOMER)
nourishment (HENRY I, TUPPER)
nuances, susceptibility to (TURNER)
nudism (CHAUCER)
nuisance (ALEXANDER, LOUIS XVIII)
Numbers, Book of, omission from
(METHUSELAH); doleful
(HERRICK); inferiority of
(AESCHYLUS)

obesity, effective treatment of
(WELLINGTON)
obligations, social, acute sense of
(PEEL)
obliquity (PLATO)
obsession (GOERING, KNIGHT,
KNOX)
occupation, sedentary (BROUGHAM)
oeuvre, chef d', biting criticism of
(SPENSER); hors d', biting of
(POE)
offence, first (SIMNEL)
Office, Holy, liberal interpretation
of functions of the (TORQUEMADA)
openness, want of (CANUTE,
WREN)
opinion, public, blindness to
obvious tendency of (BELLOC)
opportunity, quickness to grasp
(POINCARÉ)
opposition (BRADMAN)
opticians, independence of
(KNIGHT)

origin (CREIGHTON)

ostentation, contempt for (MALORY); openness to charge of (CARROLL, RANJITSINHJI)

ostracism (STUBBS)

output, literary, delusions in regard to reception of (BELLOC)

oversight (GEORGE III, PETER THE HERMIT)

pachydermatitis (RANJITSINHJI)

paint, ability to (CIMABUE); grease (BURNE-JONES); luminous, avoidance of (KNIGHT, LEONARDO); nose (ALEXANDER, BURNS, KEATS)

palaestromania (CECIL)

pariah, social (STUBBS)

pas, faux (GEORGE III)

passion, consuming (HENRY I)

pattern, cunning'st, of excelling nature, anxiety to preserve (BROWNING)

peace, total lack of interest in (HOMER)

pensée, arrière (PLATO)

percussion, instrument of, habit of treating pianoforte as (LISZT)

perversity (KELLERMAN)

pilosity (GRACE)

pique (COLUMBUS)

plantation, de ole, lub ob (BURNE-JONES)

plenitude (DANTE)

portion, dissatisfying, of genius (SHAKESPEARE)

preoccupation (GOERING, PETER THE HERMIT, WHITE)

pressing (METHUSELAH)

pretending (SIMNEL, WREN)

pride (CREIGHTON)

principle, absence of (WREN); self-sacrificing devotion to (CHAPMAN & HALL)

profusion (WALLACE)

prohibition (ALEXANDER)

promptitude (POINCARÉ)

proof (RUPERT)

propinquity (COOLIDGE, FORD)

proportion, sense of (GOERING, SAYERS, TREE); lack of (PIZARRO)

propriety (PEEL)

prostration (HOOVER); nervous, freedom from (WERNER LAURIE)

provocation (BESSEMER, CARLYLE)

prudery (YOUNG)

Prussians, distaste for (KELLERMAN)

publicity, itch for (ATTILA, CECIL, INGE)

puellis, nuper idoneus, presumption on having been (BEDE)

pulchritude (PETRONIUS)

psychology, complex and baffling, of contemporary genius (MARCONI)

Quakerish, dislike of appearing (KELLERMAN)

quality (ATTILA, CREIGHTON)

qualms, freedom from (STUBBS)

quandry (ALEXANDER, GRACE)

quantity (HENRY I, WALLACE)

quarantine (IBSEN)

queenhood, lavishness in the matter of (HENRY VIII)

quenching (ALEXANDER, BURNS, KEATS)

querulity (BRADMAN, COLUMBUS, WELLS)

quickening, spiritual, need of (WREN)

quietus, administration of, suitability for (RUFUS)

quotient (HUGO)

race (CREIGHTON)

rapture (ATTILA)

refinement (PEEL, PETRONIUS, YOUNG, WELLS)

regret (HERRICK)

remuneration (CARROLL, LEONARDO, TUPPER)

repartee, witty and pungent, gift of (BESSEMER, BOSSUET, CIMABUE, HIRST)

repudiation (SMITH)

research (GRACE)

resemblance, confusing physical, sometimes noted among higher types of genius (MAHOMET)

resolution (BURNS)

Restoration, lax morality of, readiness to fall in with (WREN)

retribution (STUBBS, TORQUEMADA)

reverie (BROUGHAM, GOERING, HUGO)

rhyme, nursery (ROSSETTI)

Rome, the grandeur that was, detraction from (DOMITIAN); enhancement of (PETRONIUS); satisfaction with (BELLOC)

ruin, road to, avoidance of the (FORD)

'rumpty tiddledy umpty ay', refrains such as, eschewment of (POE)

ruthlessness (BRADMAN)

Salvation Army, sympathy with methods of (LISZT)

Satanism, revolting display of (WREN)

scene, change of, liking for (ZINGHIS KHAN)

self-effacement, public-spirited (CLIVE)

self-respect (PETRONIUS)

sex-appeal, allergy to (KNOX)

Sheffield Wednesday Football Club (STUBBS)

sight, telescopic (KNIGHT)

simultaneity (LOUIS XI)

snow, perpetual, distaste for (SAYERS)

sorrow, secret (JOYNSON-HICKS)

space, waste of (GOERING)

statesmanship, qualities of: anticipation of coming problems (HARLEY); freedom from insomnia (EDWARD THE CONFESSOR); readiness to sink own prejudices in interest of common weal (FULLER ACLAND-HOOD)

sternutation (IBSEN)

stupefaction (ALEXANDER)

style, frigidity of, sometimes attributable to pre-natal influences (HUME)

suction (KEATS)

superfluity (JOHN, WALLACE)

superiority, effortless (CREIGHTON)

surname, non-disclosure of (PETER THE HERMIT)

taboos, faithful observance of (ODO, PEEL)

taciturnity, of the strong, silent man (BEIT)

tact (TREE)

tactlessness (GEORGE III)

Tail-Waggers' Club (STUBBS)

tarantism, immunity from (COMTE)

Tartuffe, willingness to regard, as moral exemplar (WREN)

taste, agreeable (HANNIBAL); exacting (SHERMAN); questionable, aversion from anything in (CARROLL, PEEL)

tat, tit for, aptitude in administering (BESSEMER)

teeth, indefensible recourse to (INGE)

temperament, artistic, the: its acute sensitiveness (VAN EYCK); deliberate eccentricity (FIFE); drunkenness (ERASMUS); high value set upon it by Frenchmen (TIZIANO); irresistibly attracted by the sublime (GRIEG); love of violent action (LISZT); naïve self-appreciation (CIMABUE)

theatroplegia (BEDE)

thoughts, funereal, predisposition to (HARLEY)

thrift (FORD)

tick, refusal of (LEONARDO)

time, closing, disapproval of (ALEXANDER); doing, philosophic approach to (PEACE)

timing, defective (METHUSELAH)

Timonism (WELLS)

tolerance (PEACE, SWIFT)

transferability, desire for (TURNER)

Treasury, Parliamentary Secretary to the, anxiety to remain (FULLER ACLAND-HOOD)

trial, hour of, fortitude in (FULLER ACLAND-HOOD)

tricks, monkey, practically total abstinence from (COMTE)

trop, de, openness to suspicion of being (JOHN)

turpitude (WREN)

Uffizzi, Palazzo degli, failure to be *persona grata* at (DANTE)

Ugh! (STUBBS)

ugly, indifference to appearing (WELLINGTON)

'Ulalume', alimental basis of (POE)

umbrage, quickness to take (COLUMBUS, ERASMUS)

umpire ?, how's that (GRACE)

Unaussprechlichen, Kundgebung des (BRAHMS)

understatement (RUPERT)

undervaluation (SHAKESPEARE)

unproductiveness, reproach of, freedom from (WALLACE)

unrest (BRADMAN)

unseemliness (GEORGE III)

unsung, determination not to be (KELLERMAN, SHERMAN, WELLINGTON)

untruth, plausible, ability to frame (WREN)

uplands, taste in (SAYERS)

utilitarianism, charms of, susceptibility to (MILL)

Utopian conditions, ill-judged efforts to realize (PIZARRO)

uxory (HENRY VIII, IBSEN)

Valhalla, precipitate eagerness to qualify for (SHAW)

values, nice sense of (PEEL, MUSSOLINI)

variety, thirst for (BENN, HENRY VIII)

Vaticanism, display of blighting effects of, upon human mind (LISZT, PIZARRO)

vegetable, guarded allusion to (PLATO)

velleity (TURNER)

veracity, departure from (WREN)

vertigo, liability to (SAYERS)

Victorianism (YOUNG)

view, the long (KNIGHT)

viperishness (STUBBS)

vision, double (DANTE)

vitamins, carelessness about (MACHIAVELLI, TUPPER)

vivre, savoir (POINCARÉ)

vocative, subtly offensive avoidance of (BESSEMER)

vulgarity, intolerance of (PEEL)

washes, vanity of human (CHAUCER, POPE)

watchword, ill-chosen, insistence upon (ROOSEVELT)

water-cure, inexperience of the (ALEXANDER)

wave, brain (HERRICK)

wawls, appealing, deafness to (TORQUEMADA)

waywardness, discouragement of (BOSSUET)

wear, gents', fastidious taste in
(PETRONIOUS, SAVONAROLA)
weir, ghoul-haunted region of,
preference for (POE)
Whigs, keen party spirit of,
freedom from (FOX)
width (HENRY VIII)
wilderness, sojourning in the,
distaste for (BENN)
wing, conquest's crimson, capacity
to clip (KELLERMAN)
witherin' conventionality, unspiled
by (SHERMAN)
wood-notes wild, native, unfair
competition with (SHAKESPEARE)
Woolsack, alternative to the
(BROUGHAM)
Wootton Bassett Darts Club
(STUBBS)
world, the next, neglect of
prospects in (WREN)
wranglership, senior, inability to
attain (JOYNSON-HICKS)

xanthopsis (CARLYLE)
xebec, command of, temperamental
incapacity for (TURNER)
xenophobia, selective (MUSSOLINI)
Xenophon Club (STUBBS)
Xmas, failure to merit gifts at
(WREN)

Yahoos, censorious treatment of
(SWIFT)
yarning, infinite capacity for
(WALLACE)
years, early, forgetfulness of habits
inculcated in (MARCONI); neglect
of educational opportunities in
(JOYNSON-HICKS)
yellowishness (CARLYLE)
YMCA, unfitness for (WREN)
York, metropolitan see of,
disqualification for (STUBBS)
young, forever, forever panting
and (BEDE)
youth, lost, illusory recapture of
(BEDE); misspent, evidence of
(METHUSELAH)

Zealand, New, indifference to
natural beauties of (TURNER)
zealous pursuit of pleasure at
expense of soul (WREN)
zealotry (BOSSUET)
Zeus, defiance of, inherited
predisposition to (CREIGHTON)
Zingari, I, membership of
(RANJITSINHJI)
Zion, outcast from (WREN)
zoilism (SPENSER, STUBBS)
Zulus, social practices of,
progressive lapse into (FIFE)